DARK SISTER: Poems

By

Linda Rodriguez

ISBN 978-1-939301-66-6
Library of Congress Control Number: 2018931202

Author photograph by David Joel, used with permission.
Cover photograph by Denise Low
Cover design assistance by Blue Heron Typesetters, 808 W. 8th Street, Silver City, NM 8806

Mammoth Publications is an independent, Indigenous-owned literary press, founded in 2003. Information and orders: mammothpubs@gmail.com
www.Mammoth.Publications.net
Mammoth Publications 1916 Stratford Road Lawrence, Kansas 66044

The author appreciates the following publications where some of these poems have appeared:

About Place Journal, "I Give You to River"; *ABQ Arts*, "Getting Right"; *Ariel*, "Love Takes Us"; *Coal City Review*, "At the Stomp Dance"; *Heart's Migration* (Tia Chucha Press), "Oklahoma Poem"; *Imagination and Place: An Anthology* (Imagination and Place Press) "Where I Come From"; *Kansas Leadership Center Journal*, "Tallgrass"; Letterpress broadside (Alliance of Artist Communities), "Horned God"; *New Letters on the Air* (Nationally Syndicated Public Radio Program), "Oklahoma Poem"; *Pedestal Magazine*, "Crow Mother"; *Plume*, "Class War in the Magazines"; *Present Magazine*, "Ofrenda"; *Primera Página: Poetry from the Latino Heartland* (Scapegoat Press), "The Things She Gave Me"; *Rabbit and Rose*, "At the Stomp Dance"; *The 5-2*, "Trickster Time"; *The Kansas City Star*, "Spell for Banning a Book"; *The Más Tequila Review*, "Getting Right"; *The Pedestal Magazine*, "March 19" (in an earlier form); *The Red and the Black: An Anthology about Profit and Loss* (Helicon Nine Editions), "Getting Right"; *The Whirlybird Anthology of Kansas City Writers* (Whirlybird Press), "Indian Removal Cartography"; *To the Stars: A Kansas Renga in 150 Voices* (Mammoth Publications), "To the Stars Through Difficulties"; TRIVIA: *Voices of Feminism*, "God of Hawks," "What Crow Says," "What Oak Says," "What Owl Says," "What River Says," "What Coyote Says"; *Voices and Visions* (Alliance of Artist Communities), "Dark Sister"; *Wordcraft Circle of Native American Writers and Storytellers Newsletter*, "Something to Do with Respect"

This book is dedicated to my ancestors, those I knew in the flesh and older ones I've known only as spirits.

Thank you, my elders, for your constant presence and guidance in my life and work.

ACKNOWLEDGMENTS

This book had its beginnings in a remarkable workshop at Macondo led by Marjorie Agosín and Ruth Behar. Comments by them and by Richard Blanco, Margot Chavez-Charles, Rachel Jennings, Toni Margarita Plummer, Celeste Mendoza, Levi Romero, and Vincent Toro helped me set my course in new, unfamiliar terrain. Many thanks to all the Casa/Hearth/Diaspora folks and to the Macondo Foundation.

A first draft of this book was written during a month-long residency at Ragdale, and I would like to thank the Ragdale Foundation and the Ragdale staff for their support, as well as the Alliance for Artists Communities and the Joyce Foundation for making this stay possible.

I am grateful for a research grant, the ArtsKC Fund Inspiration Award, that allowed me to travel to Tahlequah, Oklahoma, to do research and consult historical records. I am truly appreciative of the generosity of the Cherokee Heritage Center Archivist, Tom Mooney, and the Special Collections Librarian at Northeastern State University of Oklahoma, Dolores Tichwy, in sharing their time and expertise with me. I also thank Maura Garcia for proofreading my Cherokee.

As always, my husband, Ben Furnish, and youngest son, Joseph Rodriguez, have been my first readers and support team.

Linda Rodriguez

CONTENTS

1. Mixed-Blood

WHERE I COME FROM

I come from crocheted dishrags
and hand-me-down clothes from cousins
on the "good" side of the family.
I come from canvas cotton sacks (200 pounds for an adult
"but you're a big girl now, eleven,
you can pull enough cotton to fill that ol' sack"),
from Lifesavers and Nehi Orange
and salty peanuts dropped into sweating-cold bottles of RC Cola
and traded among us kids for back rubs
when we couldn't quite stand up straight after a day in the cotton rows.

I come from the heady, dangerous ozone smell
of summer thunderstorm nights
when I walked alone across town
to buy my mother's cigarettes.
I come from rain-soaked redbuds and lilacs and irises,
from mesquite and cottonwoods,
from beachfront bougainvillea and date palms.
I come from drive-in movies and drunk fathers and mothers
and singing in the church choir
and stone-headed stubbornness.
I come from Sequoiah and John Ross,
from "Cielito Lindo" sung everywhere
(I thought to me since it had my name in it),
from driving out in the dark to see the desert bloom after a rain,
from altruism and diabetes.

I come from "get your nose out of that book"
and "if it'd been a snake, it'd bit me"
and Grandpa's sermons in the pulpit on summer Sunday visits.
I'm from the Great Smokies and Tahlequah and Broken Arrow,
from Highland crofts and Dublin slums and England's younger sons
from San Diego and Coronado and El Cajon,
I come from snob dodgers and frybread for breakfast
and from fried chicken I helped kill and clean for Sunday dinner.
I come from the month the money ran out—
even my illegal paycheck from the drugstore after school—
and the grocer wouldn't give more credit,
when some angel left a bushel basket of turnips
on our kitchen doorstep.
I come from Aunt Joan and Uncle Glyn on their dirt-poor farm

who took us in on a moment's notice,
six kids deserted by both parents,
and raised us with our four cousins
in that house the size of my living room
with never a cent or a thank-you.
I come from those dark nights on the mattress on that kitchen floor,
waking to take little ones to the outhouse in the dark,
from cooking for harvest hands and combine crews
while Aunt spent the day on the tractor with the men,
from her dark Indian spitfire and his tall, Indian peace.

I come from all the photos of us kids in places all over the country
where Dad dragged us around like a tail behind him,
from all the photos of the five babies after me
and the photos of all of us with grandparents and cousins
and my school photos from San Diego, Kenosha, Arlington,
and so many others I don't even remember,
stored only in my brain, except for the handful
Aunt Joan saved for me all those years until we found each other again
when Uncle Glyn was dying in his quiet way
and cousin Dickie's abused son, raised by his grandparents,
bussed and hitchhiked back from the Navy to sleep
on the floor at the foot of Uncle's bed like a faithful hound.

I come from my grandmother's Cherokee teaching stories and
stubborn strength,
from that grandfather's wild goose chases and big dreams and fine talk,
from my other grandmother's domestic fussing
and ambitious nurturing,
from that grandfather's preaching and Bible values,
from my father's hatred of his Indian half and tolerance toward
everyone else,
from his bright, inquiring mind, his hope for humanity, and his
drunken violence,
from my mother's cold beauty and rewriting of the past,
from the short tragedy of her life,
and the strength with which she bore it.
I come from a long line of male preachers and teachers,
drinkers and dreamers,
from conjure women, curanderas, women with the Sight,
and women who survive and make do.
I come from fallen gentry and half-breed hill trash, from parsonages
and trailer courts.

I contain all of these,
and I choose,
I say,
who I will be.

OKLAHOMA POEM
for Jim Barnes

In his first words, I can hear Oklahoma,
the hill country way back behind his talk
about teaching French literature in translation,
as if I have gone home, drifted back
through all the years to that childhood place I fled.

I have described it to others
as the armpit of the nation,
when I was young and not long free
of its windy roads and redbud trees and overgrown
hills, still hurt and bitter
about things Oklahoma had little to do with,
beyond being the last place to stand
for a people and the place where one of them
was born and the place where he left
his wife and kids. The last two events were
what ate at me, and they could have
happened anywhere.

Only the first was unique
to Oklahoma, the old Indian territory
where my ancestors limped off the Trail of Tears
to join other tribes forced from their homes
by other ancestors of mine,
founded the Cherokee Female Seminary
at Tahlequah and a newspaper
all over again,
were finally forced to give up their lands
so rich ranchers could take the best parts
of the reservation and leave the hilly, scrub lands
to my great-grandparents, great-aunts, grand-uncles,
and Grandma.

What does any of this have to do with me now
all these years and miles away?
Me, with the broad squaw face,
as my father, from whom it came, called it?
When I hear Jim say about Oklahoma
(as one refugee to another), "We both got out,
but it's still inside—it settles in you,"

I know he's right, Oklahoma in more than his voice,
in the way he makes light of misfortune,
in his penchant for poking fun
at pretensions, his own and others'.
Oklahoma's settled in us both.
And through the echoes in his voice of its turtledoves
and winds and sky that could pull you off your feet
into infinity if you didn't have troubles to weigh you down
to the earth, I make my peace with it
and come home.

DARK SISTER

I am the dark sister,
the one with scars,
broken and mended.

I am the dream sister,
trailing shreds of night,
a herald foreshadowing.

I am the witch sister,
singing to the winds,
conjuring a storm.

I am the crow sister,
the disgraced one,
free of owners.

I am that sister,
stripped of layers of pride and shame,
become glowing cinder in the palm of a hand.

GOD OF HAWKS

Leaving Manhattan and the nursing home,
moving up out of the bowl of town at the end of winter,
fences and grasses of Konza Tallgrass Prairie
close in around the car like skin over an open cut.
I remember when my youngest took a summer class
in ecology, tramped the Konza, ate buffalo burgers.
Turn left now at the highway and head back
to Kansas City away from all this dying,
the Flint Hills soil like a bandage
that scarcely covers, leaving bare spots of jagged rock
sticking out all over. There never was enough dirt
to cover the hard, stony land. That's how the Indians found it
in the first place. Sharp flint you could break off,
cut things with, make fire with, useful hard rock in a hard land.
The spare nature of this country comforts me.
Nothing soft here, all stripped to basics.

The sky's bare as the land flowing past me,
and on fenceposts and telephone poles,
in dead-looking trees all along the way out of this land,
hawks sit in silent pride and arrogance,
red-tailed, Swainson's, sharp-shinned, Cooper's.
Raptor lover, I always watch for them
along this road, usually red-tails and golden eagles.
This is something different, all these beautiful killers
lining the highway back to my life.
Watching brown grasses with rusting fence
wires under sky threatening storm,
I feel the peace of coming to a hard place
that allows no giving way to the ache of grief.
I point them out to husband behind the wheel,
naming each bird we pass, mile after mile.
"They're your honor guard," he says, almost right.
Death is their god,
what they've come to honor.

TO BEN FROM RAGDALE

As I sit by myself in my green chair
in this room the color of fresh egg yolks
with a blue, white, and yellow quilt
on the high four-poster bed
with a tree growing around the bay window
where large wise crows hold council
and debate the depth of the snow,
the brightness of the sun,
the merits of my work—oh, let it be good!—
threading their raucous discourse
through the fertile, healing silence
of this house for writers,
silence that cushions and cradles us
and draws out words on paper that the crows
will judge—oh, please, let it be good!—
while I sit in my green armchair
in Alice's Rooms, surfeit of space
in which to read and think and write,
I need for you to know
that I miss the way your tawny hair
droops over your glasses
and bushes out over your ears
and the clear, vulnerable, frank look
of your gray-blue-green, maybe hazel, eyes.

I am happy here, alone
with my writing (and the critical crows—don't forget the crows),
and I sleep soundly alone in that big bed,
and all my needs are met by the maid and the staff
and the chef—imagine, a chef!—
except the need to brush your hair out of your eyes.

THE THINGS SHE GAVE ME

For Juana (Jenny) Gomez Rodriguez

I remember the faces of my children on summer evenings
when their *abuela* cried, "Don't leave this yard, *niñitos*,
or *La Llorona* will get you!"
Eyes huge with horror, they stared into the twilight
like two featherless owls, those harbingers of death.

¡Ay! La Llorona, the woman in white,
wandering the night in tears for the children she drowned,
looking for new little victims.
Everyone in the family had encountered her ghostly figure
or heard her wails one night or another.
More than once, I'd glimpsed her
vanishing from the corner of my sight.

Who was more terrified of such a murderous mother,
my little daughter and son or me, too young,
loving them so, but struggling to find or make a self
among the twisted cords of demands?

My own mother shared common ground with *La Llorona*,
for neglect and coldness are a kind of death
to the heart of any child. Could this struggle turn me
into ice against my own little ones?
Like them, I turned my eyes to Jenny,
born Juana in Jalisco,
mother to more than their father and *tios*.

When I married her youngest, we found each other,
the woman with only sons and the girl with no real mother.
She called me *hija*, taught me things she'd longed to teach
a daughter, the secrets of making killer enchiladas
and *pozole*, how to comfort child or man
without weakening either,
how to pray the rosary and make a novena.

With Jenny as model, how could I fear the night
and *La Llorona*'s wailing? She showed me how to live
so that those cords couldn't cut yet never broke.

Still, I came to understand grief that sent you

roaming the nights forever when Jenny finally slipped away,
leaving such a hole in the world
that surely none could survive. We did,
as we have a habit of doing, but she remains with me,
after all, in the things she gave me.

The pewter plate engraved with Our Lady of Guadalupe
on my kitchen wall, the cast-iron *placa*
on which I make tortillas (or used to),
the big lava stone *metate* her mother carried
crossing the border, along with the cutting
of night-blooming cereus whose descendants thrive
in my windowsill garden. Jenny lives on in the heart
she taught me to use instead of protecting.

I live another life now, but on rare summer nights
I can hear the sounds of weeping in the darkness
or see a wisp of white at the side of my vision
while I'm walking the dog who stiffens and growls
at nothing. *La Llorona*, go in peace. After all,
the only thing that separates us
is that best of women
and all the things she gave me.

FEAR AND GUILT: AGAINST SB 1070 IN ARIZONA

When they stop the brown faces,
the Chicanos, the Indians,
when they say, "Show me your papers!",
when only the white people walk free
without fear of being accosted
and arrested,
I want to tell them
their real fear comes from guilt.
Their ancestors killed the People,
the ones who were originally here.
They stole a continent.
Now they are afraid
that what goes around comes around.
It's the Indigenous in the mestizos coming here
that they fear, can't stand.

I am trying to swallow rage.
I am trying to remember
that my purpose is to heal
what has so long been broken.
I am trying to remember
that I know so many white people
who are outraged by this law, as well.
I am trying not to remember
the way they drove my ancestors
like cattle across the country in winter,
leaving a trail of the very young, the very old,
the too-weak-to-make-it behind in graves
scratched by hand from the frozen dirt.

And now they want us to show them proof
that we belong to the land they stole.
Does understanding the language of the heron
constitute proof of belonging?
Does listening to the wind?
Respecting the sacredness of corn?
Caring for the land?
Do they forget that the state they live in
was taken by force of arms,
that they once signed a treaty
giving full citizenship rights

to those who lived there,
that many of those brown faces in Arizona
have been there generations
longer than the earliest white faces?

It is more than I can handle, this hot anger,
this break in harmony with the world.
I must turn to the ancestors,
to the spirit world.
Give me strength and sense
to deal with this outrage.
Grant me *to hi dv*, the peace that starts within.
Help all of us draw together
to *a s qua dv*, triumph over oppressing powers.
You who were responsible for the survival
of following generations, even under conditions
that seemed to dictate that the People must die,
lend us your courage and your wisdom
as we fight against this unfair and callous law.
We will be shrewd and clever as you were.
We will not allow them to win.
Not this time.
Never again.

TALLGRASS

The prairie is a tough place.
Formed when the Rocky Mountain
rain shadow killed off the trees,
millions of buffalo grazed its big bluestem,
turkeyfoot, sideoats, switchgrass, grama, Indiangrass,
sweetgrass, prairie dropseed, buffalograss,
for millennia, but, big as a nightmare
when you encounter one up close,
the buffalo never defeated the prairie.

Summer in tallgrass lands is harsh—
blazing hot sun, only occasional rain in torrents.
Summer turns the plains into grassy desert,
but those grass roots plunge deep, deep into the earth,
some twelve or more feet under the surface.
The soil under a prairie is a dense mat
of tangled rootstock, rhizomes, tubers, and bulbs.
Those roots hold out against drought
and preserve the soil against thundering
gullywashers and toadswampers.
Summer never defeated the prairie.

Sometimes lightning strikes,
and fire races across the landscape
like water poured out on concrete,
spreading out with amazing speed and inevitability.
The prairie compensated by making seeds
that need to pass through flame to germinate.
Fireproof seeds, what an invention!
The tribes learned to set controlled fires
to bring back gayfeather, blazing star, prairie clover.
Now, ranchers burn the prairie each spring.
Fire never defeated the prairie.

As for winter, the waist- and shoulder-high grasses
triumph over the snow, spreading
large swathes of sun-colored grasses
across the scene, only occasionally punctuated
by a spread of snow along the meandering paths
where animal and human feet have trodden.
The prairie just absorbs the snow,

swallowing it down to build stronger, deeper roots
to withstand summer's hot, dry onslaught.
Winter never defeated the prairie.

Buffalo, white-tailed deer, antelope, pronghorns,
gray wolves, coyotes, bobcats, cougars, red foxes,
black-footed ferrets, badgers, shrews, skunks,
raccoons, possums, black-tailed prairie dogs,
jack rabbits, prairie chickens, bull snakes,
and the occasional human for centuries
made trails and paths through the grasses
by trampling them down or cutting their stems.
If trails are not continually maintained,
they disappear like smoke.
The prairie will always take them back.
The only thing that ever defeated prairie
was a man with a steel plow.

TRICKSTER TIME

(This is the way Grandmother told me,
as it was told to her.)

"They wanted the last of our land
so, they made us leave our mountains
with cloud shawls of blue, purple, green.
They penned us like hogs before the slaughter.
They drove us before them like a herd,
and we died as cattle all along the road.

"When we came to the place they were giving us,
it was nothing, hot, bare, with its buckboard hills.
This land was strange to us,
and we were strange to it.
My grandfather shrugged and said,
'It is a stopping place.'
We were stunted and pale from that ordeal
like trees that grow in shadows.

"Our leaders said, 'We will start again.'
We all worked hard as we could,
even though we were worn and thin
from *nu na hi du na tlo hi lu i*,
that Trail Where They Cried.

"Some could not forget and forgive.
A handful of men had betrayed the whole Nation.
Clan leaders of those who died
and someone died in each of the seven clans—
had a responsibility.
There was bloodshed.

"But we turned our energies to building,
to weave the world to harmony around us.
White men used to say
only the women among the Cherokee worked,
that our men were lazy.
But lazy could never have rebuilt
as we did with homes and newspaper and schools.

"It seemed we would be left alone finally.
Of course, that could not happen.
Yonega decided they wanted the Indian Territory, too.
It all began again, except this time
they told us it was to make us like them.
We would each have our own land.
Everyone knows you can't own the earth—
it's like owning part of the sky—
but the white man thinks he can.
Father said, 'Someday
yonega will try to put a fence around the sun.'

"Weary of false words, we knew
these men wanted our land
and intended to take it.
My father said, 'I know when I hear
the whistle of money, and when I do,
someone is always betrayed—
and he usually looks like me.'

"Their promises were rooted in sand.
They gave some of us small parcels of the reservation.
They gave some of us nothing.
They gave much of our land to *yonega* ranchers.
They said we were no longer Cherokee.
They said there was no more tribe, no Nation.
They moved many of us far from here
where we had brought forth once more
the grandfather spirits of our people.

"It was hard after that. Maybe harder than the Trail, even.
Little by little, many Cherokee were permanently lost.
Whiskey took a lot of good men and some women down,
and the world was sick and winter forever on its way.
For most of my life, we had no tribe,
according to the United States government.
But it was just one less hope. We had come through so much.
We had strong people who fought for years
to resurrect the Cherokee out of the ash of a dead fire.
In the end, they brought us to the circle of return.
We were a nation once more, and we celebrated
with an honoring of land and people.

"You must never forget.
The reason we fought and worked so hard
when dying was easier, the hope
your great-grandfather and great-great-grandmother
held before them always to keep from giving up or giving in,
was you and the children you will have one day
and the children they and their grandchildren will have.
Never forget the debt you owe to the grandfather spirits."

(And I have learned to say,
"*Wado*. Thank you.")

CROW MOTHER
for Frida Kahlo

They have a memory for faces, my pretty birds.
They are believers in vengeance.
Forgiveness is not in their DNA.
My shiny black sweethearts
will eat out the hearts of those who harm them
one day.

This is why I love them so.
They are like me
in their smart fierceness,
their desire for payback.
We who have been hurt
part our shiny black hair
down the middle,
tuck in a flower or two,
pull on layers of bright fabric
for camouflage,
and sharpen our talons and beaks
in anticipation.

I will curve my claws into paintbrushes
and carve my revenge into the souls
of those who wrong me.
I abstain from forgiveness
of grave accidents. Neither Diego nor God
shall escape me.
This is why I live on
when they are dead.
We recognize the human in the crow
and the caw at the base
of every human throat.

Come, my black beauties!
I've lost my wings, but you
can stab me with your beaks,
hundreds of you,
and hold me in the air
above life's afflictions.
Don't fear the pain you'll inflict.

It won't be the first time I've suffered
the death of *unos quantos piquetitos*.

I hadn't planned on living eternally
in that cursed America, alive
on every bottle and tchotchke,
photoshopped onto muscular bodies
in jockey shorts, the U.S.'s favorite saleswoman.
But no one knows who Diego is any longer,
except as the bastard who drove me mad.
Pierce me, my sweet little carrion eaters,
and lift me into eternal life in a cloud of bloody revenge.

GRANDMOTHER'S BASKET

I loved Grandmother's baskets when I was small.
They had intricate patterns and figures
woven into them in brown, black,
yellow, red, and orange.
She had different sizes and shapes,
used them for storage rather than display.
My favorite was in reds and yellows with a black border.
It looked to me as if it were woven of fire and grasses.

I would climb into cupboards, find one,
and ask why she didn't keep it out on a tabletop
where everyone who came in could admire it.
"These aren't the best ones," she said
as she fingered baskets that looked beautiful to me.
"We used to make them from rivercane,
which makes a better basket and dyes the best,
but they rounded us up in concentration camps
and drove us on a death march to a new land
that didn't have our old plants like rivercane
so now we use buckbrush and honeysuckle."
Grandmother shrugged. "You make do."

I asked her to teach me how to make a basket
like the one I loved with feathers of fire
along its steep sides. She shook her head.
"It's a lot of hard work.
First, we need black walnut, blood root,
pokeweed, elderberry. Yellow root's the best yellow,
but blood root will have to do.
They've dug all the yellow root
for rich people's medicines, call it goldenseal.
Got to have our dyestuffs first.
Got to forage for most of them.
It takes lots of trips, out and back,
to get enough to make good colors."

I knew I could do that and said so.
She laughed. "You've got to know what to pick
or dig or gather. It's like with my medicines.
Can't just go taking any old weed."
I pointed out that I was learning from her

about the Cherokee medicine plants. She just shook her head.
"It's not the same. I grow most of those.
Haven't taken you out for the wild ones yet."

I nagged at her for days, begging her to teach me
so I could have a basket of my own.
I had in mind that amazing fire-flickering basket.
I wanted to make one just like that.
My visit was over without her ever giving in.
I was used to Grandmother's strength of will.
I knew I would have to try harder next time.

There was no next-time visit.
My mother had always hated her mother-in-law.
Now, she won the battle to keep us away.
Our relationship poured out in letters
until my mother destroyed them,
refused further correspondence.
Years later, Grandmother wrote me—
a letter that slipped past my mother's scrutiny—
that she was making a basket
one last time for me.
I knew she was very ill,
soon to die.

I don't know who got the beautiful baskets
when Grandmother died, especially the one
that I loved when I was small.
Her sister and niece who cared for her
in her last illness, I suppose.
That's fair. My parents had divorced by then,
and my mother allowed no contact
with that family. But
a lumpy, brown-paper-bag-wrapped package
with Grandmother's shaky, spidery handwriting
arrived for me after her death.
My mother opened it first and laughed.
I stood waiting eagerly to snatch up
the last thing my grandmother would ever give me.
"Look at that," Mother said with more laughter.
"That ugly old thing's supposed to be a basket,
I think. She sure lost her knack for that
at the end, didn't she?"

When I was small and visiting, I knew
Grandmother already had arthritis
in her hands. That's probably why
she wouldn't teach me to make baskets—
because she didn't have the dexterity any longer
to make the kind she once had.
I still have that simple handled basket
of vines (probably honeysuckle).
The whole thing is dyed black.
There are no intricate patterns of flames
or anything else. It's just solid black.

I can see her plodding out to gather
butternuts for the black dye
and to pull the honeysuckle vines,
stripping off the leaves.
I can see her gnarled hands
painstakingly weaving under and over,
no fancy twills or double-woven sides.
Hard enough to shape
a shallow but sturdy gathering basket
for her long-unseen granddaughter.
All these years later
I have my own herb garden
where many of her medicine plants grow.
When I gather them to dry for teas and poultices,
I use that black vine basket.
I think it will last forever.

COMING AROUND AGAIN

A year ago, they cut off my breast,
carving out the lymph nodes
of the underarm as well.
They left me with an ugly, puckered scar
14 inches long and 3 inches wide,
raised one-half to one inch high
along its length, and another
incision 3 inches below that scar
where a length of tubing inserted
into the chest drained
blood and lymph into an attached bag
for 3 ½ pain-filled, sleepless weeks.

Death has come looking for me before this
several times. I have always tricked her
into leaving me to my life a little longer,
Scheherazade putting the random scenes
of daily living into dramatic narrative,
heightening conflict and tension,
generating suspense, embellishing
dull parts to create more spark and excitement,
adding touches of humor to lighten the mood,
a story playing out in front of her
to which she needs to know the ending
before she brings down the final curtain.
I've grown familiar with Death's face,
can read it to tell if I need to spice up the story
because she's losing interest. Old friend
and familiar, she bears no horror for me any longer.

I have seen the long view through her eyes,
the sacred labyrinth of galaxies
spinning out of control throughout the universe
pulling apart in spiral motion, eternal
dissipation of energy rippling outward
with magic like the violent change brought
by tropical storm clouds seen from the air,
galactic snake coiling around stars and planets
and black holes whirling like water
down a drain, sucking all matter and energy
within reach, voracious maws, widdershins,

sunwise, ears of creation cocked
for the song, symphony, story, vining
through the nebulae, gathering tension
and force, the vast's giant spring pulled taut,
ready to snap back into the kaleidoscope,
force of tornadoes, whirlwinds,
passing into the still eye surrounded
by the stomp dance of the stars,
Creator's medicine wheel, coming,
going, bringing, leaving, giving, taking,
moving up and down around the spiral
of time, infinity's tilt-a-whirl.

Remaining attached to this life, these loved people,
I have no wish to join the stardust spiral dance
of destruction and creation before I must.
I'll stay here in this incarnation as long as I can,
loving this insane world's dark and light moments
and the people, trees, birds around me, clinging
until the last to its chiaroscuro, yin and yang.
Still, I won't fall screaming into the void
when my time is up. I've seen the wheel of fortune
that is the cosmos. Life is circular, grinding all of us
into crumbs of creation, raw material for new wonders.
I've promised myself and lovely bony Ms. Death
I will embrace my ride on the celestial merry-go-round.
But the story's not over yet—there's at least one more chapter
before the spectacular, mystifying, completely satisfying climax.

2. Mestiza

LOST ON THE BORDER

after Frida Kahlo's Self-Portrait on the Borderline Between Mexico
and the United States

Blood lightning strikes ancient stone pyramids
Mating of sun and moon, light and dark energy
Male and female, European and *Indio*
Brief showy flower and deep immortal root
Constant shifting between
Creating organic balance
Out of elemental opposition
Laughing at death
Welcoming the spirits on wings of butterflies

Toxic clouds spew from towers
Landscaping the land around cities
with pipes and poisons
Loudspeakers and alarms drown birdsong
in the labyrinth of skyscrapers
Fleeing trucks and taxis through the maze of concrete canyons
to the amplified tick of the ever-scolding clock
Racing from task to appointment to meeting
Stainless steel masks between faces and flesh
Laughing at those who love the earth
Trampling what grows in favor of the metal and manufactured

Alien among factory executives and fat bankers with brittle wives
Lone living being in the midst of assembly lines, buses, and robots
Lost between Aztecs and Yankees
Lost between mariachis and Motown
Lost between nature and technology
Lost between passion and calculation
Lost between sun and moon

USURPING FRIDA

Frida, you suffered enough in your lifetime—
run down by streetcar and Diego—
but they won't let you rest
in any kind of peace. You're useful
to this commercial culture
that you hated so.
They use you to sell
art, books, fashion, playing cards,
tequila, underwear, anything
and everything. You're hot, girl!
Everyone wants to be you.
They want to see themselves
in you, as you.
Your look is fashionable.
The pain you painted and lived
is sexy to these hipsters and sellers of dreams
and commodities.
You are just another commodity,
a look, an image
that makes people open their wallets.
Not for the first time in your existence,
you are being used.
Still, you might be happy
that your image is so recognizable, so desirable.
That's what you always longed to be—desired.

Of course, they strip you of humanity
to render you exotic,
sexualized Other,
but then you always thought humanity overrated,
identified more with cats and monkeys,
parrots and butterflies,
dragonflies and hunted-down deer.
Perhaps you live again
in all the young women (and men)
who mimic your hairstyle, makeup, dress,
trying to be romantic or sexy or artistic
when you were only trying to be sane.

LA MALINCHE SPEAKS OF CORTEZ

I was the mother of the new world,
but before that, I was a girl sold after my princely father's death
into slavery, traded for my quick tongue over and again,
and given finally, grown-up now, a trader's bargain,
to that man with his black whiskers
poking through his tanned skin around those lips,
soft at first, then heated and insistent,
hard and cruel finally, and yet the same lips.
How did that happen?

I was flattered by his attention to my words, his requests
for advice and help. He was so driven, single-minded,
yet he wanted me
in the midst of his obsession with success and fame.
How could anyone resist that?

Many of the others thought him divine somehow, god or demon,
conquering peoples, destroying nations, changing worlds,
but I knew better, knew the scars twining his leg,
knew his back ached when it rained,
knew how to pleasure him until he lost all control,
knew what it was to hold him while he slept
after, knew he was not divine but all man.
My man, I thought.

His cruelty grew with power, and I did
what I always had, advise and help,
for surely my man did not want to become this devil,
this dark god of destruction he was making of himself.
That was my first mistake.
Why had I never noticed his profile of eagle
or vulture, his face sharper than I had seen at first,
eyes hollowed, deep angry crevices running
from nose to chin around the sneering mouth?
Once again, I was only a slave.

Nothing I had of him was actually mine, not jewels
and gold from Tenochtitlan, not love, not child.
He took them all back
and gave me like a worn-out mule to one of his underlings.
But how was I to live in peace after him?

And how was it I knew that in his last days
he would return to me in his mind,
once more becoming my man as his days grew thin
and I was long gone from his world?
He once called me his queen, his witch.
In the end he knew the truth of his own words.

OFRENDA

This is the altar I'm building
to my *calaverada*,
that madcap dance of death
my heart tangoed with you.
Boxes stacked and covered with fabric
to make a place of power
to draw you back to me.
A *calavera* of great artistry
will stand in for you, mimicking life
almost as well as you mimicked love.
I will bake you *pan de muerto* and *rosquete*,
still trying to please you,
buy finest bourbon, your favorite,
no *mezcal* or *tequila* for you,
place it next to the water, salt, and bread.
Mustn't forget the mirror and comb
so you can check your hair
of which you were always so vain.
I will slice my fingers cutting
papel picado skulls and hearts,
yellow, orange, pink and white,
and purple for pain,
to decorate the velvet of the altar.

I adorn the *ofrenda* and myself
with bright, guilt-swallowing marigolds,
chaining them through my hair,
string their petals across the ground
to lead you back. Let me light the *copal*
and inhale the sweet smoke,
trying to attract you even now,
drawing you to me. Mustn't cry, though.
"The path back to the living world
must not be made slippery by tears."
It will all be to no avail.
I can't fool you or anyone
into thinking I have finally found acceptance.
It's all too clear I would wrestle
the Lady of the Dead herself
for possession, to wrench you
from peaceful rest in Mictlan

and back into the tempest
that was us.

CLASS WAR IN THE MAGAZINES

I trace fingers across the polished wood
and linen upholstery. The sun breathes
through extra-large extra windows,
reflects from lime walls,
and gathers into the lemons piled
in a great glass bowl.
Everywhere is order, precise and clean.
I breathe deeply, taking in
the relaxed, careful scent of money.
My eyes focus on the shiny floors
and neat cubbyholes,
bountiful arrangements of fresh
roses, lilies, peonies, and dahlias
in glass and ceramic vases
in every corner on every surface.
The smell of money is light and flowers.

The toilet still running in the background,
I try to clean the broken tiles at the kitchen sink
and cover worn floors with handmade rugs.
The windows, cloudy with years,
permanently encased
in painted-over screens,
strain the light to a thin drizzle.
The smell of reality is something small
that died somewhere inside.

GETTING RIGHT

My skin no longer fits,
itches with ambition
and wanting
things.
I don't have time
to sit with people I love
and just be
together.
Sleep is restless.
I wake to lists,
things
to do or worry about.

Until my long-dead grandmother, old conjure woman
whose voice sings strongest in my heart,
resurrects inside my head,
dressed like *wohali*,
the eagle, her spirit animal.
She clicks her tongue at me,
hisses with shaking head.
"Get right," she says.
"See through the eyes of mind and spirit."

I know she's talking true,
know I've spent too much time
in my other side, in that world
of getting and spending and owning.
It's time to go back
to that first world
of belonging, being part of a whole,
u li he li s di,
joy.

I rise in the chill dark,
boil black, strong coffee in a pan,
let it burn its way down my throat,
bitter taste cleaning out
the restless ache of greed.
Then it's time.

I walk the bounds of my land,

sprinkling pinches of cornmeal
around sleeping house,
trees beginning to wake
with birds clearing throats
to greet the sunrise
as I do, singing
to the four sacred directions,
thanking, praising, blessing,
moving back into relationship,
awareness of enough,
wholeness.

"*Galun lati*, Creator,
make me right.
Let me see true again.
E li si, Grandmother, I am back
where I belong."

IN PRAISE OF GOLDENROD

I love the wild things,
plants native to this piece of earth,
purple coneflower, black-eyed Susan,
blazing star, ditch lily, bee balm,
bouncing Bet, golden bells, columbine,
mayapple, and goldenrod.
Maligned for decades,
blamed for the nasty pollen-work of ragweed,
goldenrod continued
as municipalities strove to erase it
from the landscape.
Modest yellow caps like a country girl's
from an earlier time, simple-leaved stalk—
nothing showy here but the color,
a splash of pure summer sun.

I have a garden bed devoted
entirely to the golden girls,
enticing honeybees, earth bumblebees,
azure, fritillary, monarch butterflies.
I never feed or water my carefree beauties
who multiply and bounce in the wind,
chrome-yellow shine times thirty this year.
When the sun and summer
have worn out my garden
and everything is brown or wilted,
my light-filled, bright girls
gleam under the old elm tree,
drawing every eye and wing.
Careless joy for free.

VISION

I sat alone, silent, eyes closed, breathing deep.
When I opened my eyes, thinking vision would pass me by
this time, Grandmother walked out of the tall evergreens,
came to where I sat under a winter-barren oak.
She had on eagle headdress and long gown of eagle feathers
with a shawl like feathers over it.
"Come," she said. Her shawl turned to wings,
and she flew up to a limb of the oak above me.
The headdress had swallowed her and come alive.
Grandmother's eyes looked at me
with their usual sly, knowing look
out of an eagle's face.

I stood, afraid of what I saw,
and she swooped down and carried me
up into the bare tree on the hill.
It was winter, so we could see in all directions.
Below was a highway packed
with naked people in chain harnesses
lined up like cars in rush hour
linked by long chains on either side
from one harness to the next.

Grandmother Eagle said, "Fly."
I looked at the ground beneath me.
"I might fall."
She thrust one huge wing toward the people below.
"They are afraid.
They could lift off those harnesses.
Perhaps, they could even fly.
But they are afraid."

I watched the sad lines of people on the road,
then closed my eyes and flung myself
from the branch into the air
which held me like I was floating in water,
bobbing with the slight ebb and flow of unseen currents.
I hovered by the tree
until Grandmother clicked her tongue.
"Tcha! Fly now. Fly."
As I tried to flap my bare arms,

they gathered feathers and became wings,
and I followed her swooping flight
over the chained people.
My whole body was turning eagle
as hers had earlier.
I cried out,
"What is happening to me?"
She never turned around
but led me on to higher mountains.
"You are changing into something new.
Now, fly!"

WALKING BLIND

All these years I have bumbled through the world,
molelike. Why did no one tell me
that the sharp edges of the leaves,
one on another and against all the rest
a million times over,
never repeated, always
a unique arrangement like snowflakes,
create dense textures I can almost touch?
I must restrain myself
from reaching out past passenger window
toward those massed trees so many miles away
so clearly defined against each other.

This hour-long ride for my first post-op,
my eyes are finally free
of bandages,
truly open for the first time
since my birth. I have no words,
must stare and stare through the glass
at unknown beauties in the ruby tail feathers
of a hawk circling over the woods,
that curve of beak, details I'd have missed
before the lovely young blonde took scalpel in hand
and with ultrasound suction pump and space-age
intraocular toric lens, gave me bionic eyes.

Months later, driving myself to my final post-op,
a great heron soars across my view of trees.
I am collecting green fabrics and yarns
to make a tapestry of those wooded hills.
I have 38 different greens.
I have discovered
it is not enough.

Daily we walk blind
through uncounted miracles and forget
we live in the heart of grace.

AWAKE AT THE END OF NIGHT

Praise the mockingbird singing farewell to night.
Praise the owl flying home with its mouse-feast.
Praise the beetle scurrying from sudden light.
Praise the moon sailing down to sleep.
Praise the branches whipping the house in the wind.
Praise thunder shaking windows and walls.
Praise sheets of lightning flaring across the sky.
Praise the seeds in darkest soil uncurling.
Praise the tendrils of root and stem reaching out.
Praise the worm that leaves riches in burrows behind it.
Praise the rain coursing down the brick walls.
Praise the blanket wrapping in our body heat.
Praise the sound of your even sleep breathing beside me.
Praise the body I wrap my leg around.
Praise the heavy arm thrown over me.
Praise the breath moving in and out between my mouth and yours.
Praise the spirits of the sun and moon that live within us.
Praise all things silent and hidden.

DOWN ON MY KNEES

> "I am down on my knees.
> Maybe now I can begin to learn something."
> Linda Hogan

When the time for dreams or demands is past,
when there can be no more negotiation,
when even my constant comrade on the journey,
hope, is driven away,
when my proud, erect standing
is knocked out from under me,
when all I can do is water the earth around me
with tears that come on their own volition
and not mine, their own timetable, too,
when everything I thought I held
in my hand has crumbled into dust,
when I am lost in the void,
then is the time of creation.

Imperceptible at first,
but inexorable, growing
bit by bit in the aching darkness,
transmuting pain into light
that builds a universe,
atom by atom,
with all its mess and beauty
that forces us to love,
against our will,
to come to life again,
Ouroboros with his tail
between his teeth.

SOMETHING TO DO WITH RESPECT

It was summer in a younger time.
We sat out on the flat roof of the garage,
slicing lemons and limes into our drinks,
watching stars showcased on the night's velvet.
I looked for The Boys
that Grandma told me about,
sons of seven medicine families
levitated to the stars to judge
whether we should be allowed to go on
every 52 years.
You waved the knife at me,
splattering citrus juice on my face.
"You got to forget all that old shit."
I've never forgotten,
and you, my old love, never made
your full cycle of years.
Something to do with respect.

3. Cherokee

INDIAN REMOVAL CARTOGRAPHY

It's an old map,
looks hand-drawn.
Starting in Georgia,
North Carolina, Tennessee, Alabama—
a broad swath of territory
belonging to the Cherokee
yet shrunken so
from where the first Europeans found them
that kidney-shaped province
splayed across the states
contracts
down to these thin lines
marking the paths they were forced to travel.

This old-looking map
has been modified for the modern scholar
with gray-banded place names highlighted.
When you hover a computer mouse
over one of these shaded names,
pertinent facts appear.
From New Echota, capital of the Cherokee Nation
in 1838, now a state park,
to Fort Butler, one of five North Carolina stockades
where Cherokee were held under foul conditions,
to Fort Payne, yet another
removal fort and internment camp in Alabama,
to Ross's Landing where more than 2,000 were held prisoner
and departed in three large groups
to travel to Indian Territory by water.
The Unicoi Turnpike, an ancient war and trading path,
took other groups onto the Trail of Tears,
is now designated a Millennium Trail.
Charleston, Tennessee, where 13,000 were held
for months, waiting to begin their unwilling trek
across five states in winter.
Hopkinsville, Kentucky,
Chief Whitepath died and was buried here,
remarkable for being one of the few
whose graves are known.
Hover long enough over Hopkinsville
and the screen will tell you

"Most of the thousands of Cherokees who died on the Trail lie in unmarked graves."

INDIAN TIME

"Indian Time" in Oklahoma,
it's "Mexican Time" in the Southwest,
"Black People's Time" in the African American community,
"JPT" among Jews.
All set in sharp contrast
to "Western European White People's Time,"
the standard for our world.

I may not always follow the hands of the clock—
or the red blinking digital numerals—
but I am faithful to ebb and flow
in my comings and goings,
my heart inner source of that,
systole and diastole,
now here, now gone,
now come anew,
like breath or wind.
I can time the world on my own pulse,
the longer cycle of the seasons,
or the wheel of years that is a life.

How foolish to think that time
is drawn by celestial ruler in a rigid line!
Through the years of our time in these bodies,
we get lost, wander and stray
like a river made of water and time.
We change our course,
jumping banks, leaving
old deltas dried out and useless.

The world flees down the line of the LED clock
using the very stuff of life to keep death behind
until individuals meet as strangers
on that paved straight and narrow roadway to do battle.

I emerge from a labyrinth,
my life until now,
wanderings that always come back around
the circle in a newer place yet still
part of the eternal round,
StarWoman's spiral dance of seasons.

I am faithful to my imagination,
the pulse of my mind reaching ahead
and around the corner,
while I stand with heart-pulse right here,
right now, always.

My Cherokee ancestors remind me,
"*Na quu na?*
How about now? Now is the time."
And I see my life's circular maze,
three-dimensional,
rising ever
to join the eternal spiraling
wheel of stars.

WHAT CROW SAYS

This is how gods are made.
The land is wild and free,
soil just beginning to cover the warm rock.
One day, the stone lights up
with the dreams of animals.
Out of the shining,
something other awakens.
These things happen so easily.
Nature is crowded—
everything intent on being warm.
Who knew what damage dreams could wreak?

This furless, clawless thing created
from whatever's wasted or not wanted in us,
we watched it arise
walking on two feet like Bear
but so weak and slow.
Bear can outrun a horse,
kill a deer with one blow.
It should have died but didn't.
Some tenacity kept it alive
and breeding and changing
the very world around it

We all spoke the same language
until that changed, too.
Now we're left with consequences.
Now we are the other,
everything other to this being.
We are the constant target in the crosshairs.
Now we live with the burden of being seen,
living into our observed death.
Great plans never work out.
Chaos is forever seeping in.
All it takes is a crack in creation
like this to ruin everything.

Here is a wound no spell can heal.
We've tried them all.
Not even Spider can weave us whole again.
Spoilage creeps over the whole land.

Cherish your wildness.
It's all we have left.
Live close to the edge.

WHAT COYOTE SAYS

Me, I like humans.
I know, Rat, Cockroach,
Possum, and me.
Not a prepossessing group,
I'll grant you that.
But we've thrived
among the detritus of the humans.
Man, they throw away such good stuff!

I know, I know! I hear the others moaning
about the good old days all the time.
Well, let me tell you the truth.
There's no comparison between
crawling around in the brush all day
trying to catch a chipmunk that's barely a bite
or—if you're really good or lucky—
a stringy, tough jackrabbit,
competing against every other predator out there,
and sneaking into a town
where no one can smell and hardly see
to score the leftovers from a church supper
or a ballgame's hot dogs and popcorn.
Let them try to tell you we could get that stuff
in the good old days
when it was just us,
and I'll have to pop them for a bald-faced lie.

Hunting used to be a lot of work
with absolutely no guarantees.
Now, I don't know about you,
but I like the easy way.
Scavenging suits my lifestyle.
You ought to see my den now.
I've got a velvet couch, a cell phone,
and a waterbed—all thrown away.
Chicks go for waterbeds, even now,
at least the sleazy ones do
and they're the only ones I'm interested in.
I'm hoping to score a flatscreen TV next
to replace this little portable I found in a dumpster.

Wolf's had a hard time
just because he won't adjust.
Noble and dumb!
So, the concrete's not as pretty
as the forests and prairies.
You can't get WWF in the forests,
and it's pretty damn funny,
let me tell you—almost as funny
as those presidential debates.
I know, I know! They're killing my cousins
and tacking up their skins on fences in the West.
So, take my advice—go East, young canid!
They just think we're extra-mangy-looking dogs.
None of them have ever seen a real wild animal.
They've got dance clubs and chicks
who don't know a real predator when they see one.
So,
they're messing up creation.
Big deal!
I'll thrive,
along with Rat, Cockroach, and Possum.
Let's party!

WHAT OWL SAYS

I have a reputation for wisdom
that simply comes from knowing
how to keep my mouth shut.
Some call me a harbinger of death.
I warn—I do not cause.
Because I am solitary,
I am a little closer
to that underground place
everyone fears so.
I get the news first,
you might say.
Not something everyone couldn't know
if they'd sleep like a bird
on a branch listening to the wind.
I've been involved
in a long and happy relationship
with death. After all,
we love what we recognize.

But all this makes me sound so gloomy
when I'm actually one of the few
who know how to live with joy
under the great tent of the sky.
My advice?
Keep your beak and talons sharp.
Listen for the little lives.
Strike quick and silent.
Eat your fill.

WHAT OAK SAYS

I take the long view,
as First Cousins should
but seldom do.
A wind that is no longer summer
never dismays me
for I have discovered
the constancy of change.
Some people have no gift for growing old.
They are always children
looking back from another world.
The immature is complete in itself,
but the most entire acorn
is not a patch on me.
Age has its benefits.

I never forget that I owe everything
I have or am to that pale blind taproot
that splits the rock of the hillside
and holds me secure
against the fiercest wind.
My shape is designed
by the wind and the sun
but I am held steadfast
by that blind senseless worm at my base.
Time flows down the mountain like a river,
and I stand as witness.
The wise man consults trees,
elders of the tribe of the living.
I have always advised and helped
my human cousins,
payment of an unknown debt.

I tell them what I know.
Seek the sun and growth.
Light is an invitation to happiness.

WHAT RIVER SAYS

The Cherokee call me Long Man,
yun wi gun hi ta,
because my body stretches and unravels
with my head in the mountains
and my feet resting in the ocean.
I constantly speak words of wisdom
to those who can understand me—
fewer every day.
It takes a quality of attention
fit for magicians or poets.
I have much to tell those
who expend the time and energy to listen.
I have seen so many things.
I know the history of rain
intimately, leaning on the world
to feel it on my skin
and take it inside me
to swell my body. Maybe,
they should have called me Long Woman.

I remember when
the mountains were home only to gods.
I knew your ancestors,
now tangled in the ground.
I swallowed my share and more.
I have seen innumerable generations
living into their deaths.
I am acquainted with the bones of earth,
ancient as the word of God
and stronger by far.
Men have tried forever
to change me and chain me,
but I still wander where I will
when I grow tired of being tame.
I remain the promise of tomorrow,
the hope of new growth
that haunts the night with hypnotic murmurs
and softens the edge between act and dream.

When all hope has fled,
come to me.

SPELL FOR BANNING A BOOK

First, find a censor.
This will be hard—
not that censors are rare,
but they are adept mimics.
Do not be fooled. No matter
how benevolent its disguise,
a frightened censor is dangerous.
Approach with caution.
To safely capture it
for your spell, you must circle
the censor chanting soothing
nonsense syllables.
It is meaning that terrifies
censors.

Surround the stupefied censor
with charms made from advertising
photographs of a mythical golden age—
smiling mothers
in high heels and aprons, silent fathers
keeping sentinel on horseback, sexless
children never asking
questions. Sacred to the censor,
such charms have power
to blind it.

Select the book
you want banned.
Set it outside the circle
of charms, and carefully
remove the charm nearest
so the censor can detect
the presence of an attempt
at meaning.

Protect yourself.
Enraged censors have been known
not only to ban books
but to burn them
and then press on to people.

CONJUREWOMAN SPEAKS OF UKTENA, THE CHEROKEE DRAGON

I will tell you, Hunter,
but it is not wise to ask.

The blazing crystal is called *Ulunsuti*
and is a window into the future and the past.
It is a blessing for the one who owns it
but a dangerous one
because of its great power.
To find this crystal
you must climb the mountain called *Gahuti*
in the Great Smoky Mountains
at night
alone.
There you will find
Uktena, the great
horned serpent.
His scales glow like sparks of fire.
The snake body, big as tree trunks,
has colorful circles all around the torso.
He also has wings like the great buzzard
and horns upon his head like the great deer.
Ulunsuti sits in the middle of his forehead.

Know this, however.
If you are seen by *Uktena*,
he will dazzle you so
with the bright light
of the crystal in his head
that you will run
toward his immense coils
instead of trying to escape,
and he can imitate the sound
of any human voice in your head,
including those you love most.
Even to see *Uktena* sleeping is death
of another kind—
that of your family and loved ones.

And should you survive all of this,

should you win *Ulunsuti*,
your danger is not over.
Ulunsuti must be kept wrapped in a deerskin
and hidden away in a deep cave.
Every seven days
it must be fed
with the fresh blood of small game.
Twice a year, you must kill
a deer or other large animal
and soak *Ulunsuti* in the blood.
Never forget to feed it
at the proper time,
or it will fly from its cave in the shape of fire
to feed itself on the lifeblood
of you or your family.

Great power bestows great demands.
Are you sure you want it?

THE LAST BELOVED WOMAN

Mother-clanned, the Cherokee towns,
farms, and orchards—before all were stolen
by those who forced the People
on the long dread march west—
belonged to the women,
as did the children.

In 1738, Nanye-hi was born
a daughter of the Wolf Clan,
married Kingfisher, bore two children.
During the Battle of Taliwa,
she took Kingfisher's place when he was killed,
avenged his death, rallied warriors to victory.
She became a *ghi gua*.

The *ghi gua*, or Beloved Woman,
was a title given by the seven clans
to women who had served the People
as warriors and mothers both.
Given a swan's wing and a special place in council,
the *ghi gua* even held a voting seat
on the Council of Chiefs. With their swan wings,
they had the final say
over whether the town went to war.

Today I watch women go to a war foolish as many,
often leaving babies behind to serve overseas.
Something's out of synch, though.
It's still the old men,
who've never set foot on battlefield
nor suckled a babe,
making decisions of war and peace.

Nanye-hi married again,
a white man, Bryant Ward.
Nancy Ward, the *ghi gua*, was respected
among Cherokees and settlers,
warned settlements of impending attacks
to prevent complete war,
negotiated treaties, all later broken.
At the end of life, Nanye-hi was forced

from her home by settlers she had protected,
died before the Trail of Tears.
Trying to fit the white man's mold,
the Cherokee shed their councils.
No place for Beloved Women.
Nanye-hi Nancy Ward was the last *ghi gua*.

We need women with swan wings.

GREAT GRANDMOTHER TELLS
OF THE TRAIL OF TEARS

Turtle doves murmured from the shade of shrubs,
the only sound besides the drone of bees and wasps
outside the kitchen's screen door.
Great-grandmother was making peach cobbler.
"It was before my time," she said, turning back
to the peaches and her deft knife.
"My mother was fourteen when she arrived in Oklahoma.
She lost two sisters and her pregnant mother
on the Trail Where They Cried
nu na hi du na tlo hi lu i.
8,000 of the more than 15,000 Cherokee
died on that black road to Oklahoma."

She looked away, then measured flour,
baking powder, and sugar into her big brown ceramic bowl.
With the pastry cutter, she blended lard into the dry ingredients.
"Thousands died. My mother told me.
Now I'm telling you. Never forget
what *yonega* did to us, to our family."

She wiped her hands and dipped a fork
into a teacup half-filled with milk
She sprinkled it over the flour mixture
and combined it all with the fork.
"The *yonega* had long wanted our land,
which was so fertile with the blood of Selu.
Has my daughter told you of Kana'ki and Selu,
magical parents of the People,
and how corn grew from the drops of blood
when Selu's murdered body was dragged across the ground?"

She added more sprinkles of milk
to the mixture in the bowl and stirred it in.
"We would not sell or give up our land
and move away to a place that didn't know us.
This was our home, our life.
It was our room inside the world
and belonged to all the People.
No one of us could sign it away or sell it.

"The years gathered by sevens.
A handful left for the Arkansas
because they were afraid.
The *yonega* stirred up trouble,
turning family against family
to try to get our land, but we resisted.
Our leaders said to us,
'People must be awake.
U na tse lid v-u na to ti vhi.
Think with your head instead of your feet.'"

Her eyes seemed to remember all those years back.
"This is how my mother told it to me."

> "I remember the rider in the fell of dark.
> Soldiers rounded us up like stray cattle.
> Our neighbor took his family and fled
> into the wild mountain lands
> where they could live and the soldiers could not.
> I wanted to fight, to hide in the mountains
> and come upon them like lightning.
> I wanted to be all teeth and claws,
> but my mother was carrying child, near her time.
> I saw the dawn eagle the next morning
> from inside a pen full of our people."

She took out the big pan she always used for cobbler
and laid the peach slices in it,
sprinkling them with sugar and tapioca.

> "They sent us walking that long, long trail
> with winter at our heels", she told me.
> "Not enough food. Not enough blankets.
> Hardly any wagons, and most of those
> lost to rocks or floods soon enough.
> I would look up at StarWoman at night.
> Pray for my mother and the baby to live
> until we came to the end. Sickness
> raged among us like a panther.
> We lost my two little sisters.
> The life went out of my mother after
> in the stormy winter days when memory of the sun
> seeped from our world. One morning,

she could not rise to join the line of walkers.
They refused to let us stay with her.
They forced us on with their guns,
and my father and I went
for the sake of my three little brothers—
to keep them alive."

In silence, Great-grandmother spooned
cobbler dough over the peaches
and sprinkled it with sugar, then slid it into the hot oven.

"We left them behind us like an animal track," she told me,
"the old, the very young, the weak, the sick.
This was never the way of the Cherokee,
but we had no choice.
They forced us onward in the bitter cold,
on and on, leaving our trail of dead and dying,
until we came to the Indian Territory,
a broken people.
They left us there with nothing
in a land that didn't know us,
longing for the green dawns of home."

Great-grandmother wiped her eyes
with the corner of her apron,
then filled a kettle with water
for washing up her mixing bowl.
"Still, our people held together and worked together
and made a new life for ourselves and the Nation.
We will always remember, though,
what the *yonega* did to us and those we buried or left
on that miserable trail where we cried."

She pumped well water into her dishpan,
adding hot water from the kettle,
and plunged her mixing bowl and utensils
into the hot sudsy water, began to scrub.
"And you must never forget.
Tell it to your daughters and their daughters."

LEARNING CHEROKEE

O si yo. Hello.
To hi tsu. How are you?
Di gwo ye ni u si wha. My hands are empty.
Ga do u s di hi a What is this?
Gi ga ge i. Red.
U ne ga. White.
A ma. Water.
Wa do Thank you.
Yo ne ga. White man.
Nu la. Hurry.
Ani yv wi a. The People.
Ga tli da. Arrow.
Ga yo tli ga do hi. Just a little land.
A ge hya. Woman.
A ni s ga ya. Men.
A sa no. Dress.
Qua na hlu gv ni. Peach trees.
Ga yo tli ga do hi. Just a little land.
Dlo ge si. Field.
Yv gi. Nail.
Ga yo tli ga do hi. Just a little land.
Tsa dag' sta sde sdi! Be careful!
A de la. Money.
Tla hv. Absolutely not.
Ni gad a ga do a! All your land!
Gi ga. Blood.
E hi sti yu. Pain.

4. Woman

HORNED GOD

Walking the narrow path
through mounds of snow,
cold air stinging my nostrils,
waking up my lungs,
walking with the contentment
of a good day's work swallowed whole,
heading in the dark frosty air
toward a bright-lighted room
with warm supper and companions,
movement on the periphery of vision
startles—something large.

I stop, turn slightly to my right,
eye to eye with a three-point stag.
One long, long half-second's stare,
then strong legs gathering and leaping,
bounding four feet each time,
five amazing leaps across my path
vanishing behind a large tree, supporting shrubs,
probably running straight out now
back to his home on the prairie.

I stand,
paralyzed,
mute,
breathless laugh,
wide smile,
breathing deep of the wild night.

REDTAIL HAWK

Young red-tail hawk sits on a fencepost
relishing a muskrat.
Curved beak holds the dripping body,
then lays it on the post,
holding it with talons
while the beak tears chunks of flesh
to swallow whole.

I didn't see this hunt,
though I have seen them in the past.
Soaring so far above the ground
on strong, sturdy wings
spreading out forever,
you'd think nothing smaller than a bear
could be seen. A second's hover,
then the stoop, a plummet
at astonishing speed,
driving talons and beak
into the tiny animal,
invisible to any nearby human
but target-marked
by the hawk's military sight.
Lift back off the ground
without real pause, carrying
the small body off
to enjoy in a tree or on a fencepost.

Now, she finishes her repast
and takes off, she by size,
females 25% larger than the males.
Under her wingspan,
the white wings look as if they wear
a separate cape over the shoulders
with just its dark edge apparent,
even with the belly band of darker feathers.
Heartbreaking beauty
doing aerial acrobatics overhead
for the sheer joy of it.
The exuberance of all the young.
Baby death on two wings.

MARCH 19

The sun is out. The naked ladies are up.
Tulips are trying to tell me winter is over.
I know better. I know how unstable this time is,
an untimely freeze always imminent.
Death is always waiting in the deep shadows
or where there are no shadows in the sun and sand
except those thrown by boys who want to hide in them
from the broiling heat and sullen stares and suicide bombs.

In home gardens, birds are descending after rainstorms.
Worms are being killed. It is the nature of things.
Something is being told in the woods.
If you listen, the wind will tell you,
the same wind that flings stray newspapers
and plastic bags around the neighborhood.
No one wants to hear the wind.
No one wants to hear that wind.
There is a chill edge to the wind
as it chatters through the trees.

Even on new spring days,
bad news travels through the air.
There are boxes draped in flags coming
through the air
and boys with hands and feet blown off.
No one wants to hear the wind.
No one wants to hear that wind.
Everything's betrayed and traded.
Listen.
Something is being told in the woods.
The dark is always waiting.

You have to know the sun is there
before it exists. You have to bring it into being.
Stand in the cold dark and offer corn
to the four sacred directions,
east and blue and morning,
south and red and summer,
west and yellow and wisdom,
north and white and death.
Sing *hey ya*. Let the wind carry your song

to the east to welcome the dawn.
That wind, pure and crisp.
No whisper of blood oiling sand.
No smell of ammunition and fuel.
That wind on which the dawn comes riding.
The world is waiting for you to know.
The sun is there. Bring it into being.
Listen to the blue wind.
Listen to that wind.
Something is being told in the woods.

CEREMONY FOR SOLDIERS

Now is the season when new life springs up.
It is a *da to ls dil* now,
a time of grace we have done nothing to deserve.
Now is the time of new life for these warriors
who have done everything to deserve our thanks.
They have faced down *hl v da ji*.
They have faced down the panther in the path.
They have *v le ni to nv*
They have shown their courage.

Asga Ya Galun lati, Great Spirit, Creator,
hear our prayer for these our children.
We ask this for the benefit of these *kan v wi' a*,
these brave soldiers.

Now is the time to return their hearts to their people.
Now is the time to return them to us
as they were before they left us.
They have been violent on our behalf.
Return their hearts, *Galun lati*.
Return them to us.

How about now? *Na quu na?*

They deserve the wealth that feeds the spirit.
They are coming back in all their power.
not *ni gv nh di ha*,
not power that is domination,
but the power of those who have sacrificed.

Asga Ya Galun lati, Great Spirit, Creator,
hear our prayer.
Bring them back among us as they were.

How about now? *Na quu na?*
Now is the time.

AT THE STOMP DANCE

Cars, trucks, all day coming.
First the leaders and their helpers
set up the cook shed,
clean, rake the ball and dance grounds.
Helpers from each clan
refurbish the seven brush arbors
circling the dance ground.

The women bring hot and cold dishes
from home, begin to cook and cover tables
while men build the sacred fire,
centered in the dance ground's circle
to reflect Grandmother Sun.

The crowd grows.
Flirting, catcalling between young men and women
turns into challenge. Head for the ball ground,
men grabbing ballsticks, women hands free—
all the better to rest on a hip while calling a sassy retort.
Game on, men against women,
each plays by their own set of rules
to much laughter and hooting.
The sad-eyed carved fish swimming through the air
on top of the pole in the center of the ball ground
watches benevolently
while the ball whizzes past
or—success!—strikes it.

Older women and others not playing call out
encouragement and laughing insults.
So do the older men, sitting in their lawn chairs,
sure they did it better.
All the while, final preparations continue
for the main event, the dance.
Women work on old cowboy boots,
making sure their turtleshell rattles—
handed down the chain of daughters—
are securely fastened to the split-open tops of the boots.
They try them on and stamp their feet hard
to check the sound of the pebbles in the rattles,
to make sure they won't come loose.

Children are everywhere underfoot,
watching ball game and sacred fire,
sniffing around the cook shed,
playing tag and hide-and-seek
outside the ring of clan shelters.
The elders of each clan—
Ani-Wahya (Wolf), *Ani-Kawi* (Deer), *Ani-Tsisqua* (Bird),
Ani-Gilahi (Long Hair), *Ani-Sahani* (Blue), *Ani-Wadi* (Paint),
and *Ani-Gatagewi* (Wild Potato)—
settle into each brush arbor
as the cooks call out that the food is ready.
Clan members bring food to the elders,
join them or eat with families, friends.

Now, the food is eaten and dishes cleaned.
Now, the turtledoves are calling as they nestle in to sleep.
Now, the fireflies are taking to the air with children chasing.
Now, the sun has set and the sacred fire brings back its light.
Now, the women put on their rattle-sewn boots.
Now, the old lead singer calls out the beginning,
Now, his brothers and nephews echo their response.
Now, his sisters and nieces step into the circle beside them.
Now, the women set the rhythm with their fast turtleshelled feet.
Now, the circle spirals out from the fire.
Now, the dance can begin.

TO THE STARS THROUGH DIFFICULTY

Owl, silent raptor, silhouetted against Flint Hills February moon,
bone moon, bitter month—when life force is infinitely fragile,
when cold turns blood to slow-moving slush, standing here
in these dark cedars—when even the hottest heart cools
with time's creeping, the round of years, like the stars, our origins—
when we run into bare-branched, ice-trimmed night
seeking love's heat,
longing for flame inside, fleeing the one who's fortified us
in the cooling years—
when owl warns what we must do to dodge this silent ice-death.

Breathe in
the prairie distance, the wide Kansas skies, the love beside us. Look up.
The blaze you seek spreads across the night sky.

LIVING IN AZTEC TIME

Reason in excess is tyranny.
Your name is written on my skin.
The circles of your life and mine entangle
around my limbs like snakes and come apart,
water and earth leading only to mud.
There is something beyond this
fifth and final cycle,
cat and dog.
It may be too late.

I will not turn to machines.
I am combing the hair of trees,
singing old songs of magic and love.
I will go to the desert,
where I miss my trees and sing no more.
There is something beyond this
fire and blood.

You know the old ways,
but you turn your back on them and me.
It may be too late.
I begin speaking crow.
You turn to salt in the wind.
I cry in coyote, but you are gone.
I will fly in search of forests.
There is something beyond this
living in Aztec time.

I say farewell to the ground beneath me.
I will live among the leaves,
never more touch the dirt.
Someday I will reach the hole in the sky.
It is not too late.
Your name is written on my skin.

I GIVE YOU TO RIVER

Turning to the water for release
from my troubles, from you,
I write your name in my palm with my finger,
then brush off the invisible letters
into the river currents passing at my feet.
I ask River to carry them out of my heart and mind,
carry them away from my life, remove all that darkness
that is you infesting my mind against my will,
replaying memories that were nothing
but playacting on your part,
though my heart doesn't want to admit,
tries to find reasons, excuses,
for all the deliberate pain.
I have to face it finally—there are none.
Hard to believe, but even harder to find
I still long for you.
This stubborn heart won't give up.
So, I barricade it, keep it safe from its stupid fidelity,
while I wait for River to carry out magic,
carry your name and games far from me,
set me free finally with the power of moving water,
my own inborn element,
which carves memories of trauma from the earth itself
and leaves wondrous scars.

RED LION MAN

Horses flee and forests catch fire
as you hunt after and through them
for the object of your desire.
You are hunger, craving what you don't have,
what you don't know, what you will never find,
destroying swathes in the wake of your frantic hunt,
chasing the unknown
until thirst and hunger stop you
and you devour and drink down everything in reach
and sleep fells you in mid-grab, mid-growl.

In the midst of this sleep
which can no longer be fought off
with your fierceness, overpowered
at last, you are laid out, vulnerable
in spite of claw and fang and muscle and roar.
In that moment, that which you desire
ventures from its hiding place,
looks upon you with pity and great shudders,
then flees for the coast,
for the desert, for the temple,
for the city, for any place
that offers temporary shelter or deep shadow.

Each time you survive that unguarded sleep,
your hunger, your rage grows.
They will summon groups of warriors
to hunt you and kill what they fear and flee.
It will take long, bloody battles
with many wounds and deaths before your own.
As your desperate spirit separates
from the dying flesh of your beast,
you will hear in the distance
your desired one singing a mourning song
in tones as clear as bells,
and bitterness will consume all
that is you, Red Lion Man,
this swing of the wheel.

LOVE TAKES US

Love takes us
from wing to root,
from seed to wood,
from night to rot
from bed to bone.

In the dark we find ourselves in too deep.
What has been loosed cannot be leashed.
Love will do the deed.

And life, bearing death like a seed,
enters and re-enters this river
where time and water wash
a maze of secrets.

Having the same heart,
we stray like a river,
trying to find
where sun and stars go
while we stay in the dark.

There is darkness in me.
The new moon rides the river,
clinging to every ripple,
rapid, and shallow.
What has been loosed cannot be leashed.

I conjure you
by the Star Hunter
in the core of the night.
Love will do the deed.

Love takes us
from root to seed,
from wood to wing,
from rot to bone,
from night to bed.

THROUGH THE BODY

"Sometimes the way to milk and honey is through the body."
Linda Hogan

Stop surrounding yourself with mirrors.
Turn them into windows.
Sink into a warm tub of lavender-scented water.
Count the creamy cups of magnolia blossoms.
Walk through a windy, crashing spring storm
that flashes light across the night sky
before every boom and blast of thunder.
Pick lemon balm and bruise the leaves
to fill the air with that quick, brisk scent.
Dip into homemade ice cream on a summer day
and let the rich, smooth chill slide down your throat.

We have been given all we need—
the tinkling of wind chimes brushed by a breeze,
a blue heron hunting in the shallows of a river bend pool,
spring air heavy with the sharp scent of rain to come as dark falls,
the salt of a lover's skin,
the lightest silk sliding across the breast,
the chorus of chirps and whistles that fills the trees
as birds greet the slow color of the dawn,
the sun-warmed sweetness of wild berries,
a loved hand rubbing kinks from back or neck,
the licorice air above a patch of fennel,
the shadows of old trees that wrap around the body
like a comforting shawl.

There was never any fall.
It was only a rumor.
Daily we walk, insensible,
through the garden.

www.ingramcontent.com/pod-product-compliance
Lightning Source LLC
Chambersburg PA
CBHW030529260626
47157CB00005B/1941